REDISCOVER YOUR SPARKLE

Revive the Real You and Be Rebelliously Happy Every Day

-A *Nourish Your Soul* Book-

Julie Schooler

DISCLAIMER

This book is designed to give readers some useful tips and ideas. It does not replace expert advice from medical or behavioral specialists. It is recommended that you seek advice from qualified professionals if you are concerned in any way.

This book is dedicated to my beloved, late grandmother, Marjorie Emily Hughes. Marjorie naturally radiated sparkle – fun, love and energy – each and every day.

Rest in peace, Grandma.

CONTENTS

READER GIFT: THE HAPPY20

Rediscovering your sparkle is of utmost importance.
To remind you to squeeze the best out every single
day, I created:

THE HAPPY20
20 Free Ways to Boost Happiness in 20 Seconds or Less

A PDF gift for you with quick ideas to improve mood and add a
little sparkle to your day.

Head to **JulieSchooler.com/gift** and grab your copy today.

1

SPARKLE

> 'Don't ask yourself what the world needs. Ask yourself what makes you come alive, and then go do that. Because what the world needs is people who have come alive.' – Howard Thurman

No Sparkle

- Do you feel rushed, overwhelmed, tired or stressed out?
- Have you got a fairly decent life... and still feel something is missing?
- When you look back, do you wonder where all that energy and enthusiasm went?

Where did our sparkle go?

What happened to all that fun, love and energy that was overflowing when we were young? What happened to our abundant creativity, our wonder, our innate sense of curiosity, our massive imagination and our ability to easily dream about the impossible?

Our day-to-day living now seems so serious. We are busy being busy. We are switched on all the time. We have so much to do. As a result, we feel stressed, overwhelmed and tired. Oh so tired. Yes, we have responsibilities – work to do, kids to feed, a mortgage to pay, but is this all there is to life?

We look forward to those few minutes of swiping, a sneaky sip of pinot or a long-awaited annual vacation because that is the only time we let ourselves actually have fun and properly rest.

Just because nearly everyone has lost their sparkle and it seems 'normal' doesn't make it right. You still crave it. Deep down when it is really quiet, if you let yourself, you can hear the whispers that tell you that life doesn't have to be this way.

The trouble is, how do you even start to rediscover your sparkle?

SPARKLE RECIPE

This short book has all the ingredients you need to create a delicious and simple recipe for rediscovering your sparkle. It is brimming with wisdom from top personal development gurus, positive psychology researchers and intuitive ways of living from happy souls who naturally embrace these concepts every single day.

Rediscover Your Sparkle shows how a few simple tweaks to your physiology, mindset and language have the power to take your daily life from tired, stressed and overwhelmed to being full of fun, love and energy.

This guide also cuts through the confusion around meditation, provides compelling reasons why a gratitude practice is a game changer and explains why being extraordinary is your birthright, something you are meant to be.

In a couple of hours this book gives you dozens of no- or low-cost, simple and practical tips to rediscover your sparkle. In doing so, you will revive the real you – the joyful soul that you know is in there but has been suppressed by the seriousness that you have taken on just to get through each day.

You may not believe it now, but you will move from just coping to thriving. Instead of standing on the sidelines of life, you will be dancing in the ballroom.

THE BOOK I WANTED TO READ

I am a wife, a mama of two young kids and a lifelong learner of self-help and personal development. And I am sick of feeling stressed, tired and rushed every single day! There must be a better way to live. Just because everyone seems to feel the same way doesn't make it okay.

So I distilled an avalanche of advice into 'sparkle strategies' designed specially to help busy people just like you and me to uncover our inner sparkle and remember how to love our lives once again.

More than any other book I have published to date, I truly have written the book that I wanted to read. This book is for me. I hope by putting it out in the world that it helps a few of you tired souls as well.

BENEFITS

Just think how great it will be when you rediscover your sparkle. There are so many benefits. You will:

- Bounce out of bed each morning with a zest for life
- Feel like you are in touch with your core self once again
- Gain tools to use language in a more powerful and positive manner
- Uncover how breathing the right way can change your life (yes, really!)
- Improve relationships with those around you from your positive interactions
- Take away some gratitude practice ideas, suitable for morning, noon and night
- Create happiness in day-to-day life without changing a single thing on the outside
- Reclaim all that fun, love and energy you know, deep down, you have inside of you

SPARKLE IS FOR EVERYONE

Busy people are happy to recommend this one short, easy-to-read guide. Readers are relieved that they can finally admit that they have lost their sparkle and want it to return. They are excited that there are profound yet simple ways to be the person they want to be without changing their entire life.

My promise is that if you use even a couple of the suggested strategies in this book, you will feel better, life will be fun again, and you will give the world the best gift of all—someone full of sparkle.

When you rediscover your sparkle, you become a lighthouse for those around you. You won't have to say anything directly. They will notice that your interactions are warmer. They will see that you laugh more readily and heartily. They will want to know the secret to your newfound calmness and happiness.

. . .

WARNING: FUN, LOVE AND ENERGY INSIDE!

Don't let that busy and rushed feeling, that negative emotional state and that underlying crappy mood continue to be the norm. It is a cruel and unnecessary way to live. Do not wait another restless night to read this book.

Be the happy person you want to be—not when the 'time is right', but today.

Read this book and you will immediately start to feel more light, energized and playful.

Think of this book as a low-cost luxury, a simple way to rediscover that sparkle you once had. And know that with this tiny luxury comes a bonus: the wisdom in these pages will help you be aware of how meaningful and exciting life can be, right now and for the rest of your life.

2

RECIPE

 'Knowledge is learning something every day. Wisdom is letting go of something every day.' – Zen Proverb

DANDELIONS

My three-year-old daughter, Eloise, let go of my hand. I kept walking a few paces. *What now?* I thought, irritated at the sudden stop. I had heard the bell ring and we were not even close to the school gate to pick up my six-year-old, Dylan. I had planned to be on time but a phone call took longer than I expected, I couldn't find a car park and then Eloise made a fuss about putting her shoes on. A typical day, late to school. Again.

I didn't turn around. "Come on, Eloise!" No response. She was still fascinated with whatever had attracted her attention. She eventually bounded over to me in a few steps. "Look!" She was so excited. It was a dandelion clock: the spherical seed head of dandelion that you can blow on so the white, fluffy 'parachutes' float away. She took a big breath and blew. Simple delight was evident in her face as she watched the dandelion seeds glide away.

I sighed. Looked at my watch. "Come on!" I repeated, even more sharply.

She took my hand and dropped the dandelion stalk on the ground as she marched with me silently through the school gates.

WHO IS THIS BOOK FOR?

I have written this book for me.

If you get something out of it, fantastic. But I needed to write it so I can remind myself on a daily basis that life truly is awesome.

Too many times I find myself full of anger, resentment and frustration about little things which is then followed up with shame, guilt and despondency as I know I have an extremely fortunate life and I shouldn't be feeling this way.

After all, I live in a relatively safe and abundant country, enjoy good health and am blessed with loving friends and family. I do try to be positive but if tiredness, overwhelm or stress are there – and when are they not? – my response is often less than stellar.

How can I not stop for a few seconds and share the simple pleasure of blowing on a dandelion clock with my beautiful daughter? I have lost the ability to delight in the simple things that my children find so easy to do.

I wrote this book for me, so I don't want to waste your precious time if it's not for you.

Who is this book not for?

- Someone who is truly happy and content with their life
- Negative or pessimistic people who are not prepared to change

Read this book if—like me—you:

- Feel like you are lost in the day-to-day
- Can't just settle for a mundane life on autopilot
- Have a repetitive, persistent thought of 'is this it?'
- Know there must be more to life than how you are living it
- Don't know who you are any more (or perhaps never knew)
- Want to NOT feel tired, overwhelmed, stressed out and stuck
- Have a hunger inside of you, a longing for more meaning in your life
- Want to reconnect with the core you that whispers to you now and then
- Are up for a challenge and willing to experiment a little with your life to bring back that sparkle you know you once had

Please note that if you are going through a diagnosed medical issue, chronic sickness, a life upheaval or a tragedy, there are more suitable books and resources out there to support you, although the tips in here can help as well. And if you suspect your issues may be coming from a more serious cause—perhaps an undiagnosed mental or physical illness—I don't want to diminish the seriousness of your situation. Please seek appropriate professional advice.

Still here? Great!

Let's get this party started.

. . .

WHAT IS 'SPARKLE'?

There is no dictionary definition for sparkle in the context that it's discussed in this book. There are some great synonyms - vivacity, animation, liveliness, vitality, exuberance, verve, high spirits, zest, effervescence, enthusiasm, vigor, spiritedness, dynamism and fire - but nothing truly captures sparkle.

It's easier to describe its opposite. It's obviously not the stress, tiredness, overwhelm, frustration and irritability I seem to have in spades.

It seems nebulous, but, like a sturdy umbrella in a downpour, you know when you have sparkle and when you don't. My daughter has an abundance of sparkle. I do not.

My definition of sparkle is anything that highlights or emphasizes fun, love and energy.

Rediscovering your sparkle means remembering how to have fun in a way that is right for your life. It involves finding out what you love the most and doing more of it. Sparkle also helps to revive your energy with activities that light you up.

Bringing more fun, love and energy into our lives is a critical thing to do yet we dismiss it, turn away from it or ignore it. We have the best excuses for not accepting more sparkle in our life but do they really stack up? More on that in the next chapter. For now, let's assemble a recipe for sparkle.

S-P-A-R-K-L-E INGREDIENTS

The letters in the word 'sparkle' are a perfect framework to rediscover your sparkle. The seven 'ingredients' in the 'S-P-A-R-K-L-E' acronym will help you tap into ways to love your life on a more consistent basis.

Each ingredient has three suggested strategies to bring about more fun, love and energy into your daily life. These are explained further in the next few chapters, but here is an outline:

Savor

Play

Appreciation

Rest

Kindness

Lightheartedness

Extraordinary

RECIPE FOR SPARKLE

Here is the recipe to help you rediscover your sparkle:

- Mix together savor, play, appreciation, rest, kindness and lightheartedness
- Add a generous dollop of fun, love and energy through suggested strategies
- Bake in some acknowledgement of just how extraordinary you really are
- To create a delicious life you absolutely love

You don't need to be a Michelin-star chef to cook this. It's an incredibly simple recipe yet it's not easy. None of these ingredients of sparkle may seem fresh to you but are you deliberately nourishing yourself with them in your daily life?

The title of this book starts with 'Rediscover' rather than 'Find' for a reason. Isn't it great to know that the recipe for sparkle is simple wisdom that you can reintegrate back into your life?

I could have made this book much longer but I wanted to get to the good stuff! I agree that we need to change our negative thoughts, regulate our emotions, revise our bad habits and address the limiting stories we tell ourselves. In my book *Crappy to Happy*, I delve into these areas.

But as author and podcaster, Gretchen Rubin says, "The absence of feeling bad is not enough to feel happy–you must strive to find sources of feeling good." Please, by all means, investigate these matters but why not adopt a few of the sparkle elements into your life as well? Why wait?

Let's tap into what makes us sparkle right now.

Let's build ourselves up, give ourselves the utmost indulgence and care and then address the mindset shifts that help us to improve our lives even more. Yes, we need to work on ourselves but why not try this as a starting point? A focus on rediscovering our sparkle will make our life brighter and is very likely to lead to some of our negative behaviors effortlessly falling away.

But... I Want More!

We had sparkle as children, but as time wore on, we grew up, became more serious and were heaped with a bunch of responsibilities. Our sparkle faded away.

The elements discussed in this book are sufficient to bring back your sparkle but they are also only the first rung or two on the ladder to a richer life. Attributes such as curiosity, wonder, courage, empathy, dreaming big, believing in the impossible, creativity, easily cultivating friendships, intuition, imagination, not worrying what others think and pure joy were in abundance in my childhood but now they have almost vanished.

First, we need to go back to basics before we try and access these loftier concepts. Savoring leads to wonder and curiosity. It is hard to use your creativity when you haven't let yourself play. And it is almost impossible to access your intuition unless you give yourself space to rest. You won't dream big if you don't embrace the extraordinary human you are.

Sure, we all have some of these traits left but they are not nearly as plentiful as they once were. I am creative enough to write a book but it's been a long while since I have completed 15 artworks with complete joy and abandon each and every day like my daughter does at kindergarten. And I set goals but have lost some of the imagination and dreaming big that my son has, like, for instance, when he tells me all the gifts he wants for his birthday.

It's easy to think these traits are a childhood indulgence, not appropriate for adults to focus on. But deep down we know that these intangible qualities are what makes life worth living.

Concentrate on the simple sparkle suggestions first and watch as they unlock all the other 'childlike' attributes that we long for. The recipe for sparkle is a gateway to our grander ambitions.

ALL ABOARD!

The next chapter will go over the objections raised against rediscovering sparkle. These may seem reasonable, however they are... well, they are just garbage. The following six chapters will discuss the main ingredients of sparkle, which lead to the final chapter and seventh element – living an extraordinary life.

In each chapter, a variety of suggested strategies will be presented to help you revive your sparkle. These will relieve pressure and boost you up so you can face the day. The sparkle strategies are meant to help you and not stress you out! If you feel overwhelmed, note that they are merely suggestions. Choose what seems most delicious to you and try it out. Many are not about adding stuff but about eliminating something nasty from your life.

I am not going to advise you to *Eat Pray Love* around the world. These are mostly low-cost suggestions to help you enjoy your life as it is right now. You really can be happier without changing your life in a drastic way.

The chapters end with three challenges that reflect the suggestions to improve your sparkle. Implement ones that resonate the most with you for a day or a week. Then, if you wish, add them into your life in a way that feels right. Assess how you feel afterwards and if you don't feel even a little more sparkle, go back to how you were.

SPARKLE MOVEMENT

Rediscovering our inner sparkle means getting right back to the basics, finding ourselves and appreciating what we truly love once again. This is so critical that I want to generate a sparkle movement. Through my book, *Super Sexy Goal Setting*, I am seeking a goal-setting revolution, so why not a sparkle movement as well?

I would love a whole bunch of people to deliberately take action that invokes their sparkle each day.

Can you imagine a world where even a tiny percent of us did that? Even 1% more sparkle in the world – wouldn't that be better? How much lighter it would it feel? How much more fun, love and energy would be cascading around us?

I want to create a sparkle movement.

I hope that you will join me.

3

OBJECTIONS

 'The mass of men lead lives of quiet desperation.' – Henry David Thoreau

NOVELS

I read not one, but two disappointing novels over the festive break. This is not the most tragic thing in the world, but it stung more than I thought it would. Why was I so bitter about reading a couple of mildly unsatisfying books?

The main reason was that I had heaped way too much anticipation onto the two novels. They were unlikely to have ever stood up to my gold-standard expectations after months and months of almost solidly reading non-fiction.

Don't get me wrong; I do enjoy non-fiction, very much. But I love novels too and I had tipped the scales far too much in one direction. In the past few years, I very rarely let myself 'indulge' in reading fiction even though it makes me really happy.

Why would I not do something that I absolutely relish?

ROLLERCOASTER

We can all agree, at least in theory, that rediscovering your sparkle is a good thing for ourselves, our loved ones and humanity, yet there is a lot of resistance to it. I understand this. Boy I do! I have raised every single one of these objections in its various forms.

This chapter will be a rollercoaster but by the end of it you will be able to glide seamlessly into the best ways to rediscover your sparkle.

Strap yourself in.

OBJECTION 1 – SELF-INDULGENT

Reading novels, especially since I had kids, seemed like an indulgence, a frivolous and almost selfish waste of time. In other words, I decided that reading for fun was not that important to me. After all, I'm a grown up and novels were just another childhood luxury I must relinquish.

One of regrets from the book, *The Top Five Regrets of the Dying* is "I wish I had let myself be happier." Yes, it may seem strange but we CAN choose to be happy. Every single day.

The very fortunate get to attain some happiness in their work, but if this is not the case then we can notice what makes us happy and lean into that. It may not be reading novels, but you will have something you currently think of as an indulgence, something you think of as a bit frivolous, maybe even selfish.

Do that thing.

Do it today.

And if you don't know it yet, there are plenty of opportunities to figure it out during the rest of this book.

Objection 2 – Too Busy

You may not come right out and say that you are too busy to be happy, but this objection can be expressed in other ways. You may say that you don't have spare time or that your family or work is your priority right now or that you are too exhausted to contemplate yet another thing you should do at the moment.

Somehow, I led myself to believe that I was too busy to do one of the handful of things I absolutely love to do most in the entire world – reading novels.

And yes, of course, like you, I lead a big, full life, but I often slide into prioritizing things that do not contribute to any real, lasting happiness. Instead of reading a book I can find myself watching a banal sitcom, shooting off an email so I can keep my inbox down and scrolling, scrolling, scrolling. Sometimes all at the same time.

Maybe I cannot lose myself in a novel on a rainy Sunday afternoon for hours at a time like I did when I was younger. But I can still go to bed a half hour earlier or read a book on my phone in five-minute increments while waiting in line.

We all have the same 24 hours in a day, and someone out there is swimming under a waterfall, learning how to juggle or strumming their favorite song on an acoustic guitar and you are not. Are you busy being busy without adding value into your life? Our culture celebrates busyness! Don't confuse this with living a fulfilling life.

Please stop lying to yourself that you are too busy - or too tired from being so busy - to bring a bit of sparkle back into your life.

OBJECTION 3 – NOT BUILT FOR IT

Some people say they can't rediscover their sparkle as they are simply not that happy and never have been. Here is the truth – being happier is harder than not being happy. Let that sink in for a moment.

Every single human on the planet has a negativity bias. Due to our need for survival in prehistoric times we had to be on alert for anything that may harm or kill us. We are on constant alert for attack or lack. Our conditioning means that we are more likely to notice the negative than the positive. This is our default position, so we have to train our minds to notice and accept the joy that is prevalent in the world.

There is this pervasive cultural belief that happy people are just the lucky ones, born with genes that allow them to be happier, always able to look on the bright side. They naturally have a sunnier disposition without having to work on it. And yes, there is some science around a 'happiness set-point' and some people do find it a bit easier to be happy, but that does not mean that it's not achievable for the rest of us. There is still plenty of leeway for us all to tap into more happiness.

First, however, you have to stop lying to yourself that you are just not built for it. Not being supremely happy is not our fault – our minds are not designed that way – but it is our responsibility. And now you know that, you can't go back.

OBJECTION 4 – DON'T KNOW HOW

The objection that you don't know how to be happy is a little sneaky as it will let you believe that you want to rediscover your sparkle but you don't know how to attain it so it's probably not worth pursuing.

Would you say that you really want that vacation but don't want to call the travel agent or learn how to book the flights yourself so you won't go? Would you say that going on vacation is too hard? You can poke holes in this 'don't know how' excuse very quickly.

Happiness is not something that happens to us; a lot of the time we have to cultivate it. Being happier is hard work but that is what makes it worthwhile.

Okay, can we now all agree that doing things that make us happy is important, that you could find room in your busy life for some more sparkle and that even though you are not built to be happy you are willing and able to find out how to create more fun, love and energy in your life?

Let's get more candid and admit that what is stopping us is not the tactics or the how-to but our mindset. On the surface, it may seem strange to have fears attached to something that seems so desirable, but it's perfectly natural. After all, now we have to admit that something is missing from our lives and we want it back.

OBJECTION 5 – FEAR OF STANDING OUT

Any time we strive for more, for something we really want, there is fear attached. One way this shows up is a fear of attack. For instance, we don't want to stand out, be different or make a fool out of ourselves in our quest for more sparkle. We want to be 'normal' but keeping to society's standards means a mediocre existence as we default to negative thinking unless we work at it. You wouldn't be reading this book if you were content with that.

Yes, rediscovering your sparkle means showing up, embracing your weird self and being enthusiastic about life, even if others judge you. I constantly have to remind myself that I would rather remain uncool yet exuberant than part of the downbeat in-crowd any day of the week.

OBJECTION 6 – FEAR OF NOT DESERVING IT

Our fears stem from our prehistoric minds. Attack – if I show my sparkle, people may judge me. Lack – in pursuing sparkle I may lose something else.

I have a recurring negative thought pattern that tells me that I don't really deserve the peak level of happiness that reading a novel can bring me.

There is a bug in my system that constantly reminds me that since others have such real tragedy and horror in their lives, and my life is fairly fortunate, then who am I to strive for soul-filling joy? I tell myself that I have 'enough' and so shouldn't want for more.

However, as Bronnie Ware explains in *The Five Regrets of the Dying*, we don't have to feel guilty about happiness – "it is a lighter feeling that we all desire."

A few weeks ago, I entered an online competition to win a pile of novels – and, just like that, I won it. This could be just plain luck, but I would like to believe it was the universe telling me that not only was it acceptable, but absolutely essential to read more fiction this year. When nine novels literally land on your doorstep, it does make you reassess what you thought was true.

Rediscovering your sparkle is about desiring, not about deserving.

OBJECTION 7 – FEAR OF EMOTION

We can now admit we want sparkle back in our lives. We desire it, we crave it, we need it. But here is the main roadblock: rediscovering your sparkle will get you to *feel* once again.

Going on this journey means getting back in touch with our positive emotions. This is hard because anyone who seems truly happy can be considered at best, naïve and at worst, certifiable. How can anyone be happy when the world is on fire?

Even more challenging: by allowing in the positive emotions, we also have to feel the so-called negative emotions – you can't feel just one type of emotion. And once you let yourself feel, you will feel everything. Everything.

You will feel sad that you didn't do this sooner, angry that you missed out on the delight and wonder of life for so long and scared, so very scared, that once you regain your sparkle you could lose it again. It's something you have denied yourself of for so long and now you don't want to let it go.

We are so used to numbing and distracting ourselves these days that acute emotions – of any type – are avoided at all costs. After all, no one likes to cry during a performance review or get the giggles at a committee meeting. Being in touch with your emotions puts us in a vulnerable state and this can be incredibly uncomfortable.

I understand this. The world breaks my heart. I care about too many things. How can I strive to live with sparkle when there is child slavery / domestic violence / plastic filling the oceans / corrupt politicians / tigers disappearing off the planet? It's all too much. What do I focus on? What is more important? How can I help when I can barely get through the day? I can't even pick up my child from school on time so tackling climate change seems a little out of my league.

As I write this book, a horrible tragedy has occurred here – 51 lives lost in a senseless and horrific mass shooting that has shaken my tiny country and the whole world. How can it even be possible to write a book about rediscovering your sparkle when there is so much hate in one person that it would cause him to carry out such an atrocious act? How can I think anything I do makes a difference?

I simply want to rediscover my sparkle so if my daughter shows me a dandelion clock again, I will stop and appreciate it. But maybe, just maybe, if that person had reconnected with his core self and found something he could focus his love on, this massacre wouldn't have happened.

Rediscovering your sparkle doesn't mean that you will suddenly deny all the horror and hurt in the world. It means tapping into all of your emotions – both 'good' and 'bad'. It is boldly seeing all the trauma and suffering yet not letting it suck you in and consume you as well.

Pursuing your sparkle means deliberately and bravely trying to be happy.

Admit that you are making excuses that are stopping you from rediscovering your sparkle. And then move forward. Please, please, please, do things that make your heart sing, things that light you up. Do them even if you still believe these objections. Do them because you read a book today that told you to.

. . .

YOUR COMFORT ZONE

People think they don't want to leave their comfort zones, as they feel nice and familiar, and they feel safe and in control of their environments. Going to work, coming back to your home, watching TV, these are all nice at times. Being in your comfort zone is comfortable, but after a while it actually starts to hurt you. You start to feel unenthused and jaded with your routine existence.

The real magic happens outside of the comfort zone. If the magic happens outside, why do you want to stay inside? Your negative and misleading thoughts tell you that it's impossible to live the life of your dreams.

Let's get this straight right now: you are responsible for your life; you create your life. Not the latest political scandal, not your current family drama, not a nuclear threat. You. If you are just going through the motions in life controlled by fear, then it is up to you to find a way to change. Don't let the story you tell yourself stop you from being truly happy and fulfilled.

The challenges that are coming up in the next chapters will deliberately try and get you out of your comfort zone of crappiness and launch into an uplifting place. For the first baby step however, you don't need to leap for euphoric joy. Instead, practice stepping out of your comfort zone with some neutral tasks. This will help train your brain to not default to its usual, mostly negative patterns.

CHALLENGES

Try these for a day or extend them out to a week so you can feel, and move through, some of the difficult emotions associated with stepping out of your comfort zone.

Challenge 1 – Replace the current ring tone for your mobile phone

Challenge 2 – Set the radio station onto one you never normally listen to

Challenge 3 – Put on a different top, socks or watch - something you rarely wear

4

SAVOR

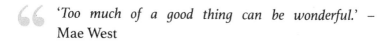 *'Too much of a good thing can be wonderful.'* – Mae West

SNAILS

Becoming a mama has changed the whole course of my life and has been the most challenging yet magnificent thing I have ever done. I have learned a lot about myself, being a parent and balancing (juggling?) everything. I expected there to be a steep learning curve in all these areas.

What I didn't anticipate is how having kids has helped me find out what is truly important in life. My children remind me on a daily basis to live life to the fullest. I may be the one imparting knowledge but they divulge the real wisdom.

A few months back, when I picked up Dylan from school, he ran off with his friends to look at a snail. Yes, a snail. When I joined him, after finishing a conversation, more than five minutes later, he was still poking around that poor snail, trying to cover it with a leaf and feed it some crumbs. Eloise was marveling at the creature as well.

As adults, we don't do this. We don't savor. We almost never 'stop and smell the roses', and so miss out on the awe and delight that savoring can invoke. Children remind us that the world around us is full of wonder and I, for one, want to make sure I remember that.

MINDFULNESS VERSUS SAVORING

Oh, you say, you are talking about mindfulness. We are told to be mindful all the time. We just did a mindfulness seminar at work. I know I should practice mindfulness more often. But you know how it is. Busy and all that.

Yes, I do know how it is! We are 'shoulding' all over ourselves! I don't want you to feel like you 'should' do this. I want you to WANT to do this.

This is mindfulness but with a sparkly twist.

Please hear me out.

Mindfulness is a trendy concept these days, but it simply means bringing your attention to the present moment. It has exceptional benefits: it is linked to improved focus, better performance at work, more positive emotions, increased self-knowledge, higher self-control and greater empathy amongst many other things. This sounds great but to rediscover your sparkle I think we can go one better.

Savor means 'to delight in / enjoy' (Merriam-Webster Dictionary). It is not just about noticing but extracting enjoyment from the moment or activity for as long as you can. Savoring, or its associated words, luxuriating, reveling, marveling, relishing or basking are simple methods of finding pleasure in everyday moments.

Doesn't savoring sound a lot more exciting than being mindful? Mindfulness is hugely important, of course it is. It's just that savoring, well, it's more fun. It may be a slight language variation, but let's go with it.

We agree that savoring sounds incredible so why don't we savor more? We are constantly distracted by our phones, rushed by our hectic schedules, future focused and want to 'save time'. These are cultural constructs that we don't have to buy into. Saving time, for instance. What does that even mean? What do we 'save' it for? Instead of saving time we need to savor. Savor not save. See what I did there?

Each sparkle element can be incorporated into our lives in a multitude of ways. This book features three suggestions for each. Some help you eliminate the excess that blocks our sparkle. Others help us to gracefully allow sparkle back into our lives.

The challenges at the end of each chapter will invite you to incorporate these suggested strategies into your life. They should feel like a welcome addition, something you didn't realize you were craving all along, that easily slots into your routine.

You can read these chapters in any order and take actions on any of the suggestions as you wish but I advise to simply follow the path laid out for you. After all, if you have not taken delight in a snail in the past few decades then you need to start at the beginning.

SAVOR STRATEGIES

1. Eliminate Distractions
2. Take Two
3. Savor Long Time

STRATEGY 1 – ELIMINATE DISTRACTIONS

With advertising blasting at us from every corner, video so easy to record and watch and the prevalence and pervasiveness of social media, we are more distracted than ever before. Did you know that we typically spend over three hours per day on our smart phones? Or that, on average, a phone is picked up an incredible 50 times per day? Or that – and this is embarrassing – 70% of us look at another device while watching TV?

It was hard enough a few years back to stay focused, but now, as Jen Sincero says in *You are a Badass*, we are so distracted it is a wonder we still speak in full sentences. This may seem obvious but in order to start savoring our real life, we must reduce our – mostly digital – distractions.

Ways to do this:

1. Turn off your push notifications. PLEASE people! You don't need the latest celebrity tweet or WhatsApp group message flickering onto your smart phone screen every four seconds. Keep your important calendar reminders on but turn the rest of them off! I am not going to tell you exactly how to do it as it is different for each device. Start by going into your settings for the relevant apps and switch any push notifications to OFF. Please. Now.

2. Do a digital declutter. Don't know where to start? Here are some ideas: unsubscribe from emails you don't need (especially those daily deal ones), delete emails that you have read and taken action on, remove apps you don't use and unfollow social media

pages, groups and people that you don't want to see in your feed any more.

3. Change your habits with your smart phone or device. Things I try to do:

- No second screen in the room while watching a TV program or movie.
- Only look at social media three times per day – once in the morning, once around lunch and once in the evening.
- Not give my phone a quick glance any time I am waiting or could be bored, like when I am standing in line, waiting for the kids to finish something or, er, at the traffic lights. If it's a short wait I challenge myself to look around. Yes, at the world. Notice things. If it's a long wait, I always have an interesting article saved or a book to read on my Kindle or Apple Books apps on my phone.
- Bonus tip: wear a watch. When I wear a watch I am not pulling my phone out to look at the time and then swiping to check something.

Yes, these are difficult at first but I didn't say finding your sparkle would be easy. I said it would be worthwhile.

STRATEGY 2 – TAKE TWO

Due to our prehistoric survival instincts, humans build neural pathways more effectively in response to negative experiences than good ones. To help our minds, we need to take a few more seconds to install the positive bits. We need to savor, marvel and bask, to slow down so our brains have time to take in the pleasure and override our natural bias to the negative.

Now we have removed (or extensively minimized) some of our major distractions, let's uncover a way to savor that is short and sweet. This suggestion costs nothing, only takes a few minutes and allows us to delight in our everyday world.

Take a two-minute break three times per day and do any of the following suggestions:

- Cloud, star or moon gazing
- Shake it all out and do a quick stretch
- Close your eyes and notice smells around you (works well in a café)
- Look up from your screen and gaze out at the view (this is good for your eyes too)
- Step outside, feel the sun on your skin and listen for the sounds of what is around you (birds, insects, traffic, talking, etc)

You get the picture. Do something that taps into your physical senses, resets you and keeps you present. It will make you feel refreshed, less alone and usually very blessed. Link 'Take Two' to another daily habit such as waiting for your morning coffee or add three alarms or calendar reminders into each day to help you to stop and savor.

An optional component of 'Take Two' is to allow yourself to sound out your savoring. Say "mmmmmm" or "wow" or whatever comes naturally to you. Sounding out savoring is a great indicator that you are basking in the moment.

STRATEGY 3 – SAVOR LONG TIME

Start with 'Take Two' and then if you are game, move onto longer activities. Here are two suggestions:

Listen to a whole album from start to finish. I am not talking about a playlist or a greatest hits compilation but one set of songs from one artist or band. Download something, pull out an old CD or dust off your vinyl collection. Put the album on when you are doing something physical like tinkering in a workshop, cooking, gardening or doing housework. Allow yourself to be swept away by the music. Dance to it if the moment takes you there.

Have a long, leisurely dinner and really take in the textures, smells and tastes of the meal. Actually chew 30 times each mouthful like your grandmother told you to do. Out at a restaurant is preferable for this, especially a very nice one that does all those little courses, but any time you eat and fully appreciate each taste is a bonus. I know this is all but impossible with young kids but maybe serve them earlier and then try it for one dinner without them sometime.

MAKE DELIGHT A HABIT

Savoring may seem like an instant gratification idea but it takes practice and dedication to make it a habit so it's a permanent part of rediscovering your sparkle. It is not skimming across a screen to whatever is the next shiny object but paying attention and delighting in the world around us.

Removing our screen obsession is important to begin to savor once again but it's even more critical when it comes to the next ingredient in the sparkle recipe – play.

CHALLENGES

Challenge 1 – Do a digital declutter in any way that benefits you the most, e.g.: remove push notifications, have an email unsubscribe-fest and delete apps that you don't use

Challenge 2 – Each day: 'Take Two'. Take two minutes, three times each day to savor

Challenge 3 – Once this week: listen to a whole album from start to finish

5

PLAY

 'Life must be lived as play.' – Plato

WATERSLIDES

A few months back, I took my six-year-old and his friend to some pop-up waterslides, set up on a temporary basis while school was out over the summertime. The boys were booked in for a two-hour session so I traipsed up the hill with them at the start and made sure they were safe and having fun. Then I retreated to the shady parents' area.

I hadn't even contemplated going with them but after a little while, I stopped being able to concentrate on my book as a little voice deep inside me kept insisting I go on the waterslides. Like, right now.

There wasn't a single good reason to stop myself so I raced to get changed into my swimsuit and headed for the waterslides. I went down at least 10 times! It was honestly the most fun I had in a very long time. It was so awesome that I was charged up, not just for the rest of the day, but for quite a while after. I truly believe that the one hour spent on the waterslides helped me get through the rest of the school holidays with a smile on my face.

And this, my friends, is the profound power of play.

NOT JUST FOR KIDS

Play is the second essential element of sparkle and yet it is so easily neglected. The thought of play can actually stress people out as it means things – important, serious things – are not getting done! We all can agree we've enjoyed playing in the past but now we are grown up it seems like a waste of time.

Even though researchers such as Dr. Stuart Brown from the National Institute of Play argue that we have a biologically programmed need for play and have listed its benefits from fostering empathy to triggering our creativity, we tell ourselves that playing is not as important as our mile-long to do list.

Charlie Hoehn points out in his fabulous book, *Play it Away* that if you dedicate 30 minutes per day to play, that only adds up to 2% of your week. When I decided to go on the waterslides, without 'too busy' to use as an excuse, I realized what stops me from playing is a bunch of fearful thoughts: that waterslide looks quite big and scary / you will look silly as one of the only adults there / you will freeze at the top of the hill while waiting to go down again / your swimsuit could come down / you could stand on something sharp while walking back up etc. We fear standing out or looking silly or hurting ourselves or not being 'good' at it. And yes, there is a risk of all these things.

But the risks of not playing are far greater: Dr. Stuart Brown argues that the opposite of play is not work but depression.

Let's see how we can incorporate more play into our lives.

Play Strategies

1. Say 'No'
2. Create a 'Playlist'
3. Schedule Play In

Strategy 1 – Say 'No'

This is for the people out there who still say they have no time to play. There is an easy fix: say 'no'.

Prioritizing play will mean some things need to be shed from your life. You need to remove the good to make way for the great. Putting boundaries around your playtime will be difficult, at least at first. If you do not learn to say no, then you are saying 'yes' to someone else's agenda and 'no' to yourself.

You can still be a lovely person and say 'no'. Author, researcher and TED speaker, Brené Brown says "Compassionate people ask for what they need. They say no when they need to, and when they say yes, they mean it. They're compassionate because their boundaries keep them out of resentment."

If you are unsure whether to say no to a future commitment, ask yourself if you would do that very thing tomorrow. Tomorrow is probably already booked up solid so if you still want to do that thing then say yes, otherwise say no. As author and entrepreneur, Derek Sivers, says "If you're not saying HELL YEAH! about something, say NO."

Even in the nicest way possible, saying no is uncomfortable, so practice on small things and build up. Here are a few ways to say no politely:

- "Sounds wonderful, but that is not part of my work focus right now."
- "Sorry but my current commitments mean I cannot take that on."
- "It sounds amazing but I wouldn't be able to give that the attention it deserves."
- "I can't help you right now but I can schedule it after X date."
- "Sorry it is not my policy to do X." (People respect policies, even ones you have made up yourself!)

If a 'no' is done well, people should be happy with how clear you are and how committed you are to what is important to you. And if they are not happy? Well, their response is their problem.

Strategy 2 – Create a 'Playlist'

I believe that all the stories we tell ourselves about how we are too busy to play or that it is a waste of time or only for kids and all the fears we let in about play are a big cover up for the actual problem about playing as a grown-up – we have forgotten how to do it.

We don't know what we like, what really lights us up, what genuine fun even is any more.

Let's face it, in today's world where we all worship at the altar of busyness and distractedness, when is the last time you had good clean fun? I don't mean finding happiness at the bottom of that glass of pinot or in the latest scroll or swipe, but in real life: the waterslide kind of fun. You need play. You have just forgotten how essential it is.

What play means to you is different to what it means to others. In *Play it Away*, Charlie Hoehn mostly defined play in terms of the traditional 'move outside in the sunshine with some friends' kind. I was stumped by this for a while. I didn't want to play catch! But then I realized that the concept of play can be broader than that.

Play can simply be thought of in terms of what you absolutely love to do: activities that bring you joy and things that are fun for you.

This is an extension of the first sparkle strategy for play: Say 'No'. We are not just making room for play but for the actual play we really want to do.

Think back to when you were a kid plus what you prefer to do as an adult in your extremely limited spare time and make a list of activities that you would like to do more of. Remember too that play can be on your own or with others. Deliberately turn toward something you want to do as opposed to 'should' do or that everyone else seems to find fun.

Writing your 'playlist' may take a while and can be added to over time. It's fine to start with the more traditional things that others enjoy, then you can cross them off later when you tap into what you truly like to do.

Here is my playlist:

- Practice some yoga / sun salutes / stretches
- Listen to and dance to music I love

- Read a great novel or interesting non-fiction book (including audio books)
- Chat with like-minded people about personal development, writing or books
- Go to a film, concert, festival or comedy show
- Walk in nature when it is fine and sunny e.g.: forest or beach
- Eat out at a nice restaurant (once in a while, not all the time)
- Visit a book store and have a good long browse
- Bake yummy treats with my kids
- Short, fun trips away with family or friends
- Fun games like disc golf, mini-golf and casual games of table tennis
- Playing Pacman on an old-fashioned arcade machine
- And of course, waterslides (at times)

You may love to do entirely different things. Here is a bunch of things I wouldn't find all that enjoyable but you may be craving to do: craft activities and scrapbooking, playing a musical instrument, painting or sculpting, hanging out with your favorite pets, team sports or playing catch in the park.

Really get down to the nitty gritty and personalize your 'playlist' just for you.

STRATEGY 3 – SCHEDULE PLAY IN

You must put play in your calendar or diary.

This goes against the spontaneous and organic nature of play but so what? If we don't schedule in time to do what we love then it won't get done.

Utilize your calendar or diary system in the best way possible. If there is one play activity you want to do this week then block out time for it. If you want to do something every day (go to bed earlier to read a novel, play a board game with the kids etc.), then get a wall calendar and 'don't break the chain'. Put a cross on the calendar for every day you take action and try to keep that chain of crosses going.

Make scheduling play a playful task. More on being playful in a later chapter.

CHANGE YOUR STATE

Play is a fantastic ingredient to rediscover your sparkle as it mostly uses your body to actively change your state. The next chapter on appreciation is a great complement to this body focus as it exercises the mind.

CHALLENGES

Challenge 1 – This week: practice saying no, at least once, in the politest way possible

Challenge 2 – Create your 'playlist' - a list of things you would absolutely LOVE to do

Challenge 3 – Schedule in a 1 x 30-minute session for play in the next week. Bonus points if you manage 30 minutes per day of play for a whole week

6

APPRECIATION

 'Gratitude is the wine of the soul. Go on. Get drunk!' —
Rumi

RAISINS

"Raisins."

This is the reply I often get from my almost four-year-old daughter when I ask her what she is grateful for. It has become a bit of an in-joke between us. I have been asking her what she is grateful for since she was two, long before she really understood the concept. Back then she often said "Raisins." I am not exactly sure why. Now she can give a wide variety of great answers but if she is feeling particularly silly or perhaps is a bit stumped, she reverts back to her usual: "Raisins".

When I do my own gratitude exercises, I appreciate that my daughter has a wicked sense of humor!

. . .

43

Why Don't We Practice Gratitude More?

Cultivating appreciation creates awareness of the good in your life and invites in some more positive thoughts that will start to nudge out some of the many negative ones. Being grateful for the small miracles of daily life—the super computer in your back pocket, the sunshine on your face, your child's laughter—makes you feel like you have enough and that your world is abundant, not lacking.

Gratitude studies have shown that an appreciation practice is associated with being more enthusiastic about life, being interested in the community, being kinder to others and getting better sleep. One study found participants were a whopping 25% happier after only a short time of practicing gratitude.

And yet many of us are not all that appreciative. Like savoring and play, we tell ourselves this is because we are too busy. A ridiculous excuse when saying "thank you" can take less than a second.

Another reason for the absence of gratitude is that we think that we don't know how to do it 'properly'. One way this 'don't know how' excuse can be believed is when there is debate about whether you are practicing gratitude or practicing appreciation and whether there is a difference between the two. It is easier to debate the semantics all day long than to simply say thanks.

Look, there may be some variation between gratitude and appreciation but I use the terms interchangeably. I called it 'gratitude' in my book, *Crappy to Happy,* but here I mostly call it 'appreciation' as otherwise it wouldn't fit in the S-P-A-R-K-L-E acronym! Choose a word that resonates with you and simply decide to be more thankful. Anything else is just a procrastination attempt to stop you from doing something that can quickly return the sparkle back into your life.

The real reason we don't practice appreciation relates to our deeper fears and worries. We think that if we acknowledge how thankful we are for our fortunate life, we will invite disaster. Won't putting emphasis on what we appreciate somehow turn our reasonably happy life upside down?

Like the other parts of rediscovering your sparkle, practicing appreciation is simple but not easy. As Brené Brown says in *The Gifts of Imperfection*, practicing gratitude can be a vulnerable act and we must tolerate some of the discomfort of vulnerability to whole-heartedly soak in gratitude or else it will be accompanied by our scarcity mindsets and fear of loss.

The absolute best way to get over the slight discomfort of scarcity fears attached to appreciation is to practice, practice, practice.

Incorporate gratitude in your daily life at any opportunity.

Here are three suggestions to do just that:

APPRECIATION STRATEGIES

1. Thank Your Bed
2. Practice Gratitude Daily
3. Massive Appreciation Exercise

STRATEGY 1 – THANK YOUR BED

I thank my bed. Yes, I thank my bed. I got this tip from Louise Hay, motivational author and founder of the publisher, Hay House. Thanking my bed is both ridiculous and profound. Ridiculous as I am thanking an inanimate object. I get a little giggle from doing it, which puts me in a great mood. It is also profound as I realize how fortunate I am to be sleeping on a bed each night. I find that most things that are worthy in life are both ridiculous and profound.

Thanking my bed is also a great way to start the day. Like many things in life, particular care should be taken with the start and end of things, with take offs and landings, and thanking your bed is a good way to 'take off'.

Strategy 2 – Practice Gratitude Daily

Endings are important, too. That is why the gratitude practices that are suggested below happen in the evening, although any time of day is good. Find a time of day and a practice that you can stick to and do it every day. It is the everyday nature of appreciation that is important, not what you do, how long it takes or even what your responses are.

Do this exercise on your own or with your partner or kids on the way to school or work, over breakfast or dinner or, especially, at bedtime.

Ask the following two questions:

- What are you grateful for?
- What are you happy about?

I often say something more profound, life affirming or esoteric for my grateful answer (the sun, clean running water, healthy kids, etc.). Then I respond with something more ridiculous or materialistic or frivolous for the happy one (my favorite TV program, chocolate or a new podcast I have discovered). You can list many things or settle on one. This is where Eloise, my daughter, comes up with 'raisins'. The answers are not important, the practice and the redirection of thoughts is.

There are many other appreciation practices you can adopt instead of, or as well as, the one above. I don't recommend taking these all on as that would be too overwhelming! Select one or two that resonate with you and make them into a habit.

- Start a gratitude list and share it via email with a few friends
- Write a list in a journal of three or more things you are grateful for each day
- Put a sheet of paper on the fridge that everyone can add a gratitude item to
- Once a week, at dinnertime, speak your appreciation to others at the table
- Create a 'Gratitude Photo Album' of images you love and keep it private or share it on social media
- If you can't get to sleep, do an alphabet appreciation exercise: think of something you are grateful for starting with A then B etc – believe me, you won't make it to Z

STRATEGY 3 – MASSIVE APPRECIATION EXERCISE

Author and entrepreneur, Tony Robbins has a method to get out of a funk and allow cheer to return after dealing with negative emotions. This brief exercise turns up the volume of positive emotions so you flood yourself with them and end up with a higher emotional baseline. It shifts your state from crappy to happy. You are not replacing the negative with the positive; you are not 'pushing it down'. The negative is gracefully released and now you are inviting the positive back in.

Give yourself three minutes for this activity. First, close your eyes, place your hands onto your heart and breathe deeply and slowly. Feel your heart's strength and power and its miraculous ability to keep you alive and well without you even thinking about it. Then think of three moments from your past (yesterday, five years ago, when you were a child or any time) that make you feel immensely grateful. Fully step into those moments and vividly remember the grace, magic and beauty of those times. Finally, think of one thing you can be joyful about right now. Perhaps your heart beating? The fresh air around you? The beautiful memories you have access to at any moment? Now open your eyes, smile and move on with your day.

Believe me, it is almost impossible to feel bad after soaking yourself in appreciation in this way.

JUST SAY THANKS

These are wonderful suggestions but you don't have to get all fancy with appreciation. Just try to say 'thank you' more throughout the day. Saying 'thank you' is a polite and easy way to bring appreciation into your life, only takes a second or two and a genuine thank you may make someone else's day.

I sent off a two-sentence email to someone thanking her for a particular podcast episode I found inspiring. When I got in contact with her again, over six months later, she remembered my kind words. She had not only told her friends and family about the email but said it had helped her continue with her podcast.

Giving her a quick thank you took me a minute and it made her whole week.

Savoring, play and appreciation are all exceptional strategies to invoke sparkle but they won't get you anywhere unless you decide to prioritize rest. It may seem dull but, as we will see in the next chapter, rest is a vital component of rediscovering your sparkle.

CHALLENGES

Challenge 1 – Thank your bed every morning straight after you wake up

Challenge 2 – Choose a gratitude practice and stick to it each day for a week

Challenge 3 – Attempt the massive appreciation exercise once this week

7

REST

 '*The amount of sleep required by the average person is five minutes more.*' – Wilson Mizener

SLEEP

When I was pregnant with my first child, I was given a lot of well-meaning advice for impending motherhood. But when it came to the recommendations about sleep, I disregarded them as I was one of those lucky people who happily thrived on five or six hours per night. I didn't think that having a newborn baby would impact on my sleep that much.

How wrong can one woman be?

There is simply no way to prepare yourself for how little sleep you may get in those first months with a newborn. I developed what I coined 'sleep stress' (try saying that ten times fast). What the books didn't say was how difficult it was to know whether Dylan would have a 15-minute catnap or sleep for three hours.

In those first few weeks, I got to the stage where I would be happy if I managed to lie down and close my eyes in a dark room for ten minutes. I also developed 'sleep jealousy'. I would get a visit from a friend who told me they had a sleep-in or an afternoon nap and I would literally see green. If someone told me that they had had eight hours of sleep in a row, I would almost break down in tears at the thought of such an unheard-of luxury.

During the nastiest times in those first few months with a newborn I actually found myself hallucinating. I thought I had a conversation with my husband but he wasn't even home. I made stupid mistakes like trying to towel-dry myself in the shower cubicle before I turned the water off.

Now that I am way past the newborn stage with both my kids, now that – knock wood – they sleep through the night, I have a much better appreciation of sleep. However, it still never feels like enough.

Why do we not allow ourselves to rest?

Not a Luxury

Rest is the least, well, *sparkly* of all the elements of sparkle but it is an absolute necessity. Without rest we simply cannot function, let alone sparkle. Sleep is not a luxury but we treat it like one. There are many reasons for this – our pursuit of more, the cultural requirement to be busy at all times and the many 'shiny object' alternatives to actual proper rest like the next must-see show that has just dropped.

I believe however that it is deeper than that. I always believe it is deeper than that! Because we have lost the sparkle in our lives, we try to make it up with things that we think will make us happier or give us some short-term pleasure or escapism but are not actually contributing to our sparkle.

We wake in the morning, race around like a lunatic all day long, finally 'get it all done' or most of it done to a point we can be satisfied or can partially ignore the next urgent task until tomorrow, then find out it is already 9.30pm and don't want to go to bed yet because we haven't actually done anything we truly wanted to do! We haven't done anything that would bring some sparkle into our day.

At this point, we are too tired to actually do something active, even something we might love like reading a book. We are certainly way too exhausted to do one of the things we 'should' do, like work on a hobby, meditate or even wash our face properly. So instead, we passively watch whatever is on and by then its after 11pm so we roll into bed, read two pages of that juicy, fat novel and fall into a restless sleep.

Er, is this just me?

If we took time to savor, play and appreciate, even in short intervals during the day, we would allow ourselves to properly rest as we have already given ourselves what we truly crave – the nourishing activities that bring us love, fun and energy.

As inspirational speaker and trainer, Alexander Den Heijer says: "You often feel tired, not because you've done too much, but because you've done too little of what sparks a light in you."

Hopefully you have started building in some of the first elements of sparkle into your life. Then you will actually want to rest properly so you can enjoy your life to the fullest. But if not, please read on and try and incorporate rest as a habit. Doing so will make the sparkle strategies listed in the other chapters even more attractive.

Please note that if you feel chronically tired, then it is worth seeking professional help. You may have an underlying thyroid, hormonal, adrenal or another issue that is not being picked up. At the very least, I suggest you read life coach, Louise Thompson's book: *The Busy Woman's Guide to High Energy Happiness* or nutritional guru, Dr. Libby Weaver's *Exhausted to Energized*.

Rest Strategies

1. Breathe
2. Meditate
3. Sleep

Strategy 1 – Breathe

We have 20,000 opportunities each and every day to boost our health and happiness—every single time we breathe.

Most people breathe shallowly, only using the upper parts of their lungs. This type of breathing keeps you in your sympathetic nervous system (SNS) and hence holds you in fight or flight mode.

It's time to relearn how to do slow, deep belly breathing. Yes, relearn—it is how babies naturally breathe. These belly, or diaphragmatic breaths invoke your parasympathetic nervous system (PNS) and hence your rest, digest and repair systems. Your body slows down and starts healing. When the PNS is active, the SNS cannot be dominant, which means it is more difficult to be on alert and stressed.

Breathe in through your nose and count to four so that your stomach gets inflated, like you are filling up a balloon. Hold that breath for a count of four. Then breathe out through your nose or mouth to a count of four and hold it for another count of four. Don't worry about the nose/mouth thing—do whatever comes naturally to you. Also, don't worry about how many seconds you take with the inwards and outwards breaths and holding it. Just make sure your stomach gets inflated, which means that your lungs are filling up with oxygen.

This is meditation teacher and wellness expert, Davidji's '16-Second Meditation'. I know you are busy, but you have 16 seconds to spare, don't you? Do this as much as you can during the day as a mini reboot to the present. It helps to link it to other daily activities like waiting for the tea to brew, showering and at a red light.

If you don't take anything else from this book, promise me that you will relearn how to breathe right. Do your own version of the 16-second meditation every day.

We have already talked about savoring – taking some short breaks during the day to drink in the fine world around you. Taking some deep breaths while you savor is the perfect way to crank up all the goodness that savoring brings.

STRATEGY 2 – MEDITATE

Meditation is an ancient practice dating back thousands of years. It has been around for millennia because it works. Maybe you tried it but felt like the imperative to clear away all your thoughts was too hard. Perhaps you couldn't commit to an hour a day. Possibly you didn't know if you were doing it 'properly'. After a time, you stopped. Now it seems like just another thing on the long to do list that you will never cross off.

You do not have to clear away your thoughts. Your job in meditation is to observe your thoughts and let them go by without judgment. You do not have to commit more time than you can fit in to meditate each day. The benefits of meditation have been shown with a practice that takes as little as three minutes per day. Meditating every day is the most important thing. You can't meditate 'wrong' unless you are checking Facebook or driving or mowing the lawn while you are doing it. For a traditional meditation practice, a quiet space where you are unlikely to be interrupted for a few minutes is the ideal, but even that is negotiable. Your subjective experience of the meditation is not that important. You may feel bored, fidgety and that you have tons of thoughts, but you still may be in a deep meditation without realizing it.

The point of mediation is to give your mind a rest. A constant practice will calm the mind and leave some space. Less chatter means a clearer head, a more focused mind and more energy. The goal of meditation isn't to control your thoughts but to stop letting them control you.

Numerous studies have shown a direct link between a consistent meditation practice (even a few minutes each day) and almost every positive health and wellbeing outcome you can think of. It has a beneficial impact on medical issues like nausea, ulcers, anxiety, even diabetes and heart disease. It has lowered pain intensity and decreased the length of the common cold. It has been shown to boost positive emotions like compassion and reduce negative ones such as loneliness in the elderly and post-traumatic stress in veterans. Meditation actually changes brain function and can help with focus, creativity and maintaining longer periods of productivity. No wonder modern workplaces are embracing it.

If you want to 'get something out' of meditation like it is some sort of transaction, then spend some more time investigating the myriad of benefits it offers. But remember there is no competition when it comes to meditation. Your own practice may improve over time, but the only 'winners' are those who commit to it every day.

Think of meditation as a little daily luxury, a treat, something you can do just for you. Give yourself permission to do nothing for at least three minutes, then try to build up to ten.

Find a meditation practice that you like and will keep doing. This may take some experimenting, and this is fine. First, find a quiet place and a good time each day to meditate. Favorites are in bed before getting up in the morning or last thing at night, in a parked car before work or in the evening straight after dinner.

It doesn't matter whether you sit up or lie down. You don't have to sit in a certain posture or lie in a particular way. You don't have to wear anything special or light candles or anything. Sit or lie so you are comfortable. If you think you may fall asleep, that is fine, especially for a nighttime meditation. If you don't want to fall asleep, then set an alarm to go off at the end of the three (or ten) minutes.

In order to let your thoughts drift through your mind, many meditation practices encourage concentrating on something in the present. One such thing is the breath, so you can concentrate on your breath going in and out. Another way to concentrate on the present is to adopt a mantra. This can be linked to the breath, for example, in breath—peace, out breath—calm. At the start, your thoughts will override this practice almost every second, and all you do is get back on track again and again: 'Oh that is a thought about the laundry, breathe in peace, breathe out calm'.

Alternatively, there are guided meditations you can follow. These can cost money and will require headphones, but may make meditating easier. You can find guided meditations all over the Internet or you can buy CDs, MP3s or download meditation apps such as Headspace.

The best thing about a guided meditation is that you can concentrate on the music or voice and not the chatter in your head. And even if you don't listen to it 100%, even if you feel your mind drift, you will still get a lot of the benefit of meditation from relaxing and breathing deeply. I have found guided meditations the easiest way to commit to a meditation practice each day.

STRATEGY 3 – SLEEP

Look, I am not going to tell you how to sleep, when to sleep or how long you should sleep for. I am not even going to suggest the best nighttime 'get ready for bed' routine, how you shouldn't have screens in your room or where to purchase blackout curtains. Goodness, I am not even going to tell you to go to bed at the same time. I do none of these things myself.

You KNOW you should get more sleep, just like you know you should drink more water, exercise daily and eat a lot of vegetables. We all know to do this stuff; we just don't do it.

Here is what I suggest – go to bed half an hour earlier each night than you usually do. That is all. That is likely to give you over three hours more sleep each week. Doesn't that sound amazing? Three extra hours of beautiful slumber each and every week. That's the equivalent of over 150 hours or almost 20 full nights of sleep in one year!

If you would prefer an actual bedtime then go to bed with lights out by 10pm. Author and speaker, Marci Shimoff calls this "catching the 10 o'clock angel train". Set an alarm on your phone for 9.30pm and when it goes off – start getting ready for bed. My night alarm says 'STOP FAFFING AND BRUSH YOUR TEETH'. Feel free to use the same wording if it's the kick up the proverbial you need to get the rest your body so obviously requires.

Encore

Let's practice belly breathing right now. With me, take a deep breath so your stomach expands out, hold it for a few seconds and then exhale it out. Doesn't that feel good?

Breathing the right way is crucial - yet perhaps a little ordinary method - to rediscover your sparkle. If you want something a bit more spectacular, keep reading as the next chapter kicks sparkle up a notch with its focus on kindness.

Challenges

Challenge 1 – Breathe – do a deep breathing exercise intermittently throughout each day

Challenge 2 – Meditate – do three minutes of meditation every day for a week

Challenge 3 – Go to bed, lights out by 10pm every night for a week

8

KINDNESS

 'No act of kindness, no matter how small, is ever wasted.'
– Aesop

My Not-So Secret Hurt

Just after Dylan turned two, we were delighted to find out that I was pregnant again. That delight turned to despair a few weeks later when I had an early-term miscarriage. Trying to make sense of my emotional reaction, I did what I always do – write. It was a cathartic way to deal with what happened. It was only after I finished that I knew I had to post it on my blog.

At that time, only a few close friends and family members knew that I had been pregnant so posting a blog about my miscarriage for the world to read was risky. But the point of the blog post ended up being a wish to open up the conversation about pregnancy loss and miscarriage so it seemed like the right thing to do.

I had absolutely no expectation as to the impact of that one blog post. I was surprised when many women opened up to me about their own experiences. A lot of people forwarded it to friends and said it helped them. And I was swamped with beautiful comments and kind wishes. One friend even left a box of chocolates with a thoughtful note on my doorstep.

One of the darkest times in my life turned out to be a wonderful way to have honest conversations, permit myself to be vulnerable and allow others to express their compassion and empathy. I didn't ask for kindness but it was ready and waiting when I needed it the most.

Why is that? I believe we have a lot of kindness inside of us that is just looking for an excuse to get out.

Top Tier

We are told that giving to others makes us happier. Of course, we know that kindness is important. We are not monsters! To be happy, we must give our joy out to the universe freely and abundantly. But when we feel rushed, tired and overwhelmed, giving is just another thing that can make us feel, at best, smug, but more often, resentful.

It helps to think of kindness in an alternative way. Give because you know your happiness counts. Give because if you are happy then others around you are more likely to be.

Give because it grants you a richer life.

Remember, you need to feel fulfilled yourself before you give. Fill yourself up with the other sparkle elements first and then attempt this top tier recommendation. Remember to do some deep belly breaths each day, meditate, express gratitude, savor life's pleasures and give time over to activities that you absolutely love and that are fun for you. Only after all that is it a good idea to give to others more than you do already.

KINDNESS STRATEGIES

1. Listen
2. Wish Happiness
3. Random Acts of Kindness

STRATEGY 1 – 'LISTEN

One simple, free way to give more is to listen to others. Like savoring, listening is a lost art. We have two ears and one mouth but we don't prioritize them in that order.

Practice active listening. Let the other person finish what they want to say, without interrupting or finishing their sentences. Look them in the eye and act interested. Then ask them at least two follow up questions on the topic without relating it back to yourself at all. If you are not sure what to ask, say these three little words: "tell me more."

Sometimes it is hard to listen actively and deliberately create constructive conversations. When we are lacking sparkle, it's all we can do not to slump and scroll. On these occasions, the best way to be kind is to simply not lead with the negative. Don't start with a criticism.

Start with adoration

Now when my kids come out of their rooms with odd socks on or ruffled hair, I try to stop myself from critiquing or tidying them up and instead, pause, smile and remind myself what teacher and author Toni Morrison says: "Let your face speak what is in your heart."

After all, kindness always starts with a smile.

STRATEGY 2 – WISH HAPPINESS

Something you can do that takes ten seconds and spreads a little loving-kindness is to 'wish happiness'. Google pioneer and best-selling author, Chade-Meng Tan describes how to do this to Tim Ferriss for his book, *Tools of Titans*.

When at work, home or out and about, identify someone and just think, 'I wish for you to be happy'. Repeat with a second or third person throughout the day if you wish. Being on the giving end of a kind thought is a happy reward for you.

In *Tools of Titans*, a woman describes how doing this loving-kindness practice once per hour for her work day produced her happiest day at work in seven years. Yes, a total of 80 seconds of wishing others to be happy made the work she detested bearable, even enjoyable, for the first time in many years.

STRATEGY 3 – RANDOM ACTS OF KINDNESS

A fun method to be kind is to practice random acts of kindness. The example often given is to buy a coffee for the person in the line behind you, but you can get lots of ideas from randomactsofkindness.org. You can do this for perfect strangers or for friends, family or work colleagues.

For instance:

- lend out a spare pen
- hold open doors for people
- send a friend a bunch of flowers
- give someone a lovely compliment
- pick up litter at the beach or the park
- offer to take a photo of a group of tourists
- leave some extra coins in the parking meter
- return someone's empty supermarket trolley for them
- provide a glass of water to the package delivery person

Look up 'random acts of kindness' and you will get a multitude of lists you can select ideas from.

It has been proven that doing five acts of kindness in a single day gives a significant boost to happiness.

No Crowbar Needed

Remember, kindness doesn't need to be forced. Put away the crowbar! Get fun back into your life and then not only will your joy bring happiness to others, but you will want to be kind and give back more to the world because you already feel so great.

The next chapter is all about harvesting even more fun from our everyday lives, so turn over for the next ingredient in sparkle: Lightheartedness.

Challenges

Challenge 1 – Practice active listening by not finishing sentences, not changing the subject back to yourself and asking at least two follow up questions or saying "tell me more"

Challenge 2 – Try the loving-kindness practice of wishing happiness silently at least once today

Challenge 3 – Do at least one random act of kindness this week

9

LIGHTHEARTEDNESS

 'Life is too important to be taken seriously.' – Oscar Wilde

DINER EN BLANC

I recently attended the sixth annual Diner en Blanc event here in Auckland. Diner en Blanc involves taking along your own picnic hamper plus small, foldable table, white chairs, white tablecloth and white napkins and then having dinner with thousands of other glamorous strangers all dressed to the nines completely in white at a secret location.

It. Is. So. Much. Fun.

The most common response is a question along the lines of "what is the picnic for?" People enquire if we are raising money for a charitable venture, whether there will be a keynote speaker or if it is part of a business? No, no and no. The Diner en Blanc picnic has been created simply for the participants to enjoy themselves. No other reason. And believe me...

It. Is. So. Much. Fun.

People say arranging to go to Diner en Blanc every year seems like hard work. They would be spot on. As the thousands of guests put in so much effort just to get there, everyone is ready to cut loose and have a grand old time.

It. Is. So. Much. Fun.

I am not saying prioritizing fun is easy. It may take some hard work and organization to participate in even the smallest fun activity, but that only makes the experience richer and more fulfilling.

PLAY VERSUS PLAYFUL

We have already talked about Play so you may be thinking what more can be added with this element of Lightheartedness? I think of play as an action, something you are doing, something you are using your body for. I think of lightheartedness as being playFUL. It is the mindset side, the BE, not just DO aspect of bringing the sparkle back into your life.

Think of the difference between Play and Lightheartedness as the difference between doing what you love and loving what you do.

Feeling cheerful and carefree when we were kids was easy but now we are all grown up, being serious is our default. Becoming more lighthearted shouldn't be so hard! We think that if we allow ourselves to stop being serious then it will all fall apart. We confuse being carefree with not caring. And we tell ourselves we are too busy or don't know how to be more lighthearted or it is only for children. Check back to Chapter Three for rebuttals to those excuses.

Let's check in on how you are. Right now, unclench your jaw, drop your shoulders and relax your tongue. Were these parts tight? How is all that tension helping us?

We care so deeply it hurts and this has translated to grim living. But we can care AND be lighthearted. Let's find out how...

LIGHTHEARTEDNESS STRATEGIES

1. No News
2. I Love That About Me!
3. Lighten Up

STRATEGY 1 – NO NEWS

This powerful suggestion stops negative and harmful thoughts from entering your mind and ruining your day.

Stop watching, reading and listening to the news.

Right now.

Stop the news.

Remove the news apps from your phone, stop the notifications, swap your newspaper with a fluffy magazine, and change the channel when the news comes on. Replace the negative input with a positive, interesting or educational one—a TED talk, a podcast, an audiobook or a funny YouTube clip. You will be amazed at how much more time you have without constant news disruptions and how much more positive you feel when surrounded by upbeat stories.

Switching off the news is not turning a blind eye to the pain and suffering in the world, but it does stop you feeling terrible about it and so adding more weight to it. And it doesn't mean you are 'uninformed'. Headlines will creep into your world regardless of how vigilant you are. Let someone else tell you the latest breaking news; give them the opportunity to inform you what is going on.

Some of you may find this an extraordinary request, but you don't need to know everything that's happening in the world, especially if it makes you feel crappy. The fact is that the news is designed to scare people. It is certainly not there to help us feel cheerful and relaxed. Trying to feel lighthearted while consuming the news is like sunbathing at night – it will never work.

Not consuming the news for a week may be hard but feeling terrible because you watched some horrible, devastating news story that you can do nothing about is even worse.

STRATEGY 2 – I LOVE THAT ABOUT ME!

We are our own harshest critics, the chatterbox in our head can be so very mean at times. Our lives never stack up to the Insta-perfect feeds we see. But how to change? Where to start? You have years, decades, of unkindness towards yourself to undo. Why not try this little mantra from author and coach, Jeannette Maw?

I love that about me!

The exclamation point is mandatory.

Isn't this simply fabulous? We are unique individuals with a variety of strengths and weaknesses. We are better at some things and worse at some things. None of us is great at everything. Our diversity is humanity's greatest strength. Let's embrace it.

The best time to use this mantra is when you feel shame, embarrassment or lack at something you can't do well. Instead of denying it, own it with lively exuberance. Just because you are 'bad' at some things doesn't make you any less of a person. Often it leads to hilarious stories and an opportunity for others to help you – i.e.: extend their kindness to you. It also doesn't mean you give up or never try to do that thing better. All it means is that next time you will attempt it with a lighter understanding of yourself.

Examples taken from my own life:

- "I snowboard like a drunken monkey" – I love that about me!
- "My four-year-old can draw better than I can" – I love that about me!
- "I couldn't use a compass to get out of my own house" – I love that about me!

Try it. Next time you find yourself in a position where you are doing something that is not your strength, don't beat yourself up – just say (in your head, muttering, or out loud and proud) – I love that about me!

STRATEGY 3 – LIGHTEN UP

One way to lighten up is to simply lower your expectations. I am not for an instant saying that you shouldn't strive to be the best person you can be. What I am suggesting is to take action, go for it, proceed and not spend too much time dwelling on the exact outcome you want.

After all, the outcome is unlikely to perfectly match what you expect. Either it falls short of what you desired, in which case you are disappointed or annoyed, OR you exceed what you thought, which makes the outcome you aimed for irrelevant.

When acting lighthearted, remember to choose your environment with care. Funerals, the court room or in airport departures queue may not be the best place to indulge in these fun practices. But please don't use that as an excuse not to attempt to love whatever you are doing.

We live in the most safe and abundant time in human history, the zombie apocalypse hasn't arrived as yet, so let's celebrate being alive!

Here are three actionable ways to lighten up:

Say YES. I know, I told you earlier to say no. I want you to say no when you feel resentment. And I want you to say YES when you may default to a no because you think you are too busy for fun or have some other poor excuse. A while back I was just leaving a friend's house when our two boys asked if they could throw around some water balloons. My default answer was a 'no' as I had to go soon but my friend said 'yes' with the caveat to throw the balloons at the fence outside and not at each other. They followed the rules and had the best time for just a few minutes. The smiles on both their faces were as wide as the sun. If I had defaulted to my usual no because of a perceived lack of time, my son would not have that cherished memory of a few minutes of carefree fun with a friend.

Make up your own rules to bring about joy. Not everything you do is going to translate into the utmost jubilation at all times, but we can learn to be happier with even the most arduous of tasks. As discussed in *Minimalism*, finding ways to transform positive experiences you dislike – especially ones that lead to growth and contribution – into positive experiences you enjoy is the ticket to long term happiness and fulfillment. Author and entrepreneur, Tony Robbins used to hate playing golf as he didn't like all the rules. Now, he loves it because he made up his own rules and goes out to smash the ball around and have a blast with his close friends. How can you make washing dishes or data entry more fun today?

Shake that ass! Put on a song and dance to it. Some call this 'a one-minute dance party'. Speaker and ultimate performance specialist, Joseph McClendon states that when you move your body you change your attitude. He calls this 'asstitude'. Stand up, move your ass and forget about your problems for a few seconds. It's been proven that dancing helps you to rewire your brain into a more productive and happier state. Put some alarms or reminders on your phone to 'shake that ass' today.

These suggestions are just the tip of the iceberg. Find your own ways to lighten up. Embrace 'Talk Like a Pirate' day. Plan a party where everyone wears mullet wigs (as suggested by investor, Chris Sacca in *Tools of Titans*). Tell a silly joke. Or simply give yourself a hug - you will look weird but you will feel good. And remember when you are down that nobody, not a single soul on the planet, can continue to be frustrated while saying 'bubbles' in an angry voice.

PATHWAY TO JOY

Adding fun back into our life allows us to say no to things that are not that important – all the distractions and multi-tasking madness. It helps to clear pathways to what really makes us happy – and isn't that what we want?

Many of us crave something sweet and think we will find it in the back of the pantry or fridge. But this craving for something sweet is not a nutritional need, it is a deep need for more light and laughter in your life. Do something nice for yourself that doesn't involve chocolate: prioritize fun and give yourself the chance to have some sweet and essential joy.

After all, as they say, there is little point of taking life too seriously as none of us make it out alive.

CHALLENGES

Challenge 1 – No news for one week - aim to not watch, listen to or read any news for one week and if your spirits improve, extend the experiment

Challenge 2 – Say "I love that about me!" next time you do something 'wrong' or 'badly'

Challenge 3 – Shake that ass - dance to your favorite upbeat song for one minute and reap the benefits of 'asstitude'

10

EXTRAORDINARY

 'Beauty begins the moment you decide to be yourself.' – Coco Chanel

GRANDMA

My paternal grandmother, Marjorie, was unreservedly and unashamedly my absolute favorite grandparent. Why? Let me tell you about her:

Grandma, despite not being able to finish high school because she had to help out her family, was one of the most intelligent and wise people I have ever met. Until a few months before her passing, she did the crossword puzzle every day. She had a love of books and read prolifically, a love that was passed down to me. It was at Grandma and Granddad's home that I first read the classic, *Little Women* and it was at their home that I read it another half dozen times.

My grandmother was really good-natured, appreciative and grateful of her life. She always said she was thankful for all the simple things – her family, where she lived and the things she had done and seen in her lifetime. After she celebrated her 80th she would say to us: "every day is a bonus."

In addition, Grandma was kind and loving. She spent almost 60 years with Granddad and often said to us: "if he had two heads, I would have married him." We always thought it was funny imagining Granddad with two heads. She would go out of her way to help those less fortunate and was active in various charities and community endeavors. I very rarely heard her say an unkind word about anyone.

I always thought of Grandma as an 'extraordinary-ordinary' human being. She didn't change the world, but with her wise, kind and appreciative traits, she made her little corner of it a great place to be.

Recipe for Sparkle (Again)

Here again is the recipe to help you rediscover your sparkle:

- Mix together savor, play, appreciation, rest, kindness and lightheartedness
- Add a generous dollop of fun, love and energy through suggested strategies
- Bake in some acknowledgement of just how extraordinary you really are
- To create a delicious life you absolutely love

All the sparkle elements and strategies lead to here.

We can now start to accept just how extraordinary we are.

Still not there yet?

YOU ARE EXTRAORDINARY

Rediscovering your sparkle is primarily about eliminating superfluous stuff from your life to bring you back to what is truly important to you. The sparkle strategies and challenges are ways for you to reconnect with your core self and embrace the extraordinary being that you already are.

Sure, these suggestions are a little uncomfortable as they make you different, make you stand out. But the truth is, you do stand out, as you are already extraordinary.

This is not nonsense.

It is fact.

Think about it – you are the only YOU that has ever existed and will ever exist in this world.

Because we have finally indulged in some much needed ME time, we are able to take a look and assess some of our triggering emotions, bad habits and stories that hold us back. Now that we have boosted ourselves up with giant, delicious helpings of sparkle, we are now able to take a breath and show up. We can do the things we are put on the planet for, take action on the goals that were just buried dreams, travel to that exotic place that has only been a fantasy or work on a long-term project that leans into your purpose.

The more you know about who you are, what you love and what drives you, the easier it will be to feel successful and fulfilled.

The planet and the universe need your special input. We need you to be the mightiest human you can be. The person you are meant to be. But if you are not at the point of striving to reach your potential just yet, know that you don't have to do something extraordinary to be extraordinary. Just deciding to face each day with cheer, to show up, to strive for happiness makes you one of the remarkable few, in a world where default living and stress is the norm. We may have fairly mundane lives, but we can still find joy in the ordinariness.

Despite the world being on fire all around us, we CAN decide to be rebelliously cheerful and content.

Allowing sparkle back into your life will lead you to other important qualities that have fallen away. Creativity, imagination and dreaming big, among other traits, stem from savoring, play, appreciation, rest, kindness and being lighthearted.

So be your unapologetically weird self, whatever that involves. Be quirky, whimsical, wonderful, irreverent, poignant, esoteric, celebratory, funny, honest, loving, joyful, or whatever makes YOU extraordinary.

This is your permission slip to return to your fabulousness. This is your permission slip to allow some jubilation in. This is your permission slip to embrace that inner sparkle.

Be happy or else.

SPARKLE DAY

There are a number of sparkle strategies and challenges listed in this book and you may be thinking, where do I start? They all seem so delicious but it is stressing me out trying to figure out how to be happier!

Here is my solution: decide that tomorrow will be 'Sparkle Day'. This doesn't replicate all strategies and challenges but creates a combo of the best parts together.

You can select whatever strategies and challenges you want for your own Sparkle Day.

Here is one Sparkle Day itinerary you can apply that incorporates an abundance of fun, love and energy for a small cost and time commitment·

- The evening before Sparkle Day, take all push notifications and news apps off your phone and make a promise to yourself not to check social media more than three times the next day
- As soon as you wake up, thank your bed (giggle optional)
- Meditate for three minutes, taking some slow, deep breaths while you do so
- Bounce out of bed and give yourself a bit of a jiggle and a stretch
- Do a one minute dance party – shake that ass – either now or schedule it in during the day sometime (perhaps after the savoring or gratitude exercises)
- Add an alarm or calendar reminder on your phone so it will go off three times during the day to remind you to stop and 'Take Two' – savor something for two minutes, taking some slow, deep breaths while you do so
- During the day, when you see someone, say in your head 'I wish for you to be happy' – try to do this at least three times
- At the end of day, ask yourself (and your loved ones if they are around) "what are you grateful for?" and "what are you happy about?" and bask in appreciation for a few moments

- Make sure you are in bed, lights out by 10pm – 'catch the 10 o'clock angel train'
- Optional: plan to do 30 minutes of play – something you really love to do – remember this is only 2% of your day

Total time commitment: less than 15 minutes without play or a total of 45 minutes with the play activity.

I don't expect you to aim for a 'Sparkle Day' every day. But I do want you to feel what it's like to live with sparkle for a day, catch hold of the best parts of it and then turn into a habit so that it can enhance your life.

At the start of the book I said that I wanted to create a sparkle movement. Any time you commit to Sparkle Day, get in contact with me and I will do it with you. This is the real start of a movement – two people deliberately striving for something better.

Simply email me: julie@julieschooler.com with the subject line: Sparkle Day.

Dandelions (Again)

Eloise recently turned four. I asked her what she wanted for her birthday breakfast and as we didn't have the ingredients to make what she wanted, I decided on the spot to have a Mama and daughter date at the local café. On our walk there, Eloise got excited, let go of my hand and scooped up a dandelion clock so she could blow the spherical seed head into the air.

My stomach growling, looking ahead at the café in the distance, I hadn't even noticed it.

This time I stopped with her and said, "Remember to make a wish before you blow."

I may not be as effortlessly tapped into my inner sparkle as my young child, but I can sure as heck embrace sparkle when it's on offer.

Our breakfast together was great, but it was this little moment that will be treasured forever.

APPENDIX

CHALLENGES

Savor Challenges

Challenge 1 – Do a digital declutter in any way that benefits you the most, e.g.: remove push notifications, have an email unsubscribe-fest and delete apps that you don't use

Challenge 2 – Each day: 'Take Two'. Take two minutes, three times each day to savor

Challenge 3 – Once this week: listen to a whole album from start to finish

Play Challenges

Challenge 1 – This week: practice saying no, at least once, in the politest way possible

Challenge 2 – Create your 'playlist' - a list of things you would absolutely LOVE to do

Challenge 3 – Schedule in a 1 x 30-minute session for play in the next week. Bonus points if you manage 30 minutes per day of play for a whole week

Appreciation Challenges

Challenge 1 – Thank your bed every morning straight after you wake up

Challenge 2 – Choose a gratitude practice and stick to it each day for a week

Challenge 3 – Attempt the massive appreciation exercise once this week

Rest Challenges

Challenge 1 – Breathe – do a deep breathing exercise intermittently throughout each day

Challenge 2 – Meditate – do three minutes of meditation every day for a week

Challenge 3 – Go to bed, lights out by 10pm every night for a week

Kindness Challenges

Challenge 1 – Practice active listening by not finishing sentences, not changing the subject back to yourself and asking at least two follow up questions or saying "tell me more"

Challenge 2 – Try the loving-kindness practice of wishing happiness silently at least once today

Challenge 3 – Do at least one random act of kindness this week

Lightheartedness Challenges

Challenge 1 – No news for one week - aim to not watch, listen to or read any news for one week and if your spirits improve, extend the experiment

Challenge 2 – Say "I love that about me!" next time you do something 'wrong' or 'badly'

Challenge 3 – Shake that ass - dance to your favorite upbeat song for one minute and reap the benefits of 'asstitude'

Sparkle Day

Here is one Sparkle Day itinerary you can apply that incorporates an abundance of fun, love and energy for a small cost and time commitment (15 minutes or 45 minutes with play):

- The evening before Sparkle Day, take all push notifications and news apps off your phone and make a promise to yourself not to check social media more than three times the next day
- As soon as you wake up, thank your bed (giggle optional)
- Meditate for three minutes, taking some slow, deep breaths while you do so
- Bounce out of bed and give yourself a bit of a jiggle and a stretch
- Do a one minute dance party – shake that ass – either now or schedule it in during the day sometime (perhaps after the savoring or gratitude exercises)
- Add an alarm or calendar reminder on your phone so it will go off three times during the day to remind you to stop and 'Take Two' – savor something for two minutes, taking some slow, deep breaths while you do so
- During the day, when you see someone, say in your head 'I wish for you to be happy' – try to do this at least three times

- At the end of day, ask yourself (and your loved ones if they are around) "what are you grateful for?" and "what are you happy about?" and bask in appreciation for a few moments
- Make sure you are in bed, lights out by 10pm – 'catch the 10 o'clock angel train'
- Optional: plan to do 30 minutes of play – something you really love to do – remember this is only 2% of your day

READER GIFT: THE HAPPY20

Rediscovering your sparkle is of utmost importance.
To remind you to squeeze the best out every single
day, I created:

THE HAPPY20
20 Free Ways to Boost Happiness in 20 Seconds or Less

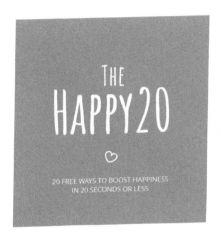

A PDF gift for you with quick ideas to improve mood and add a
little sparkle to your day.

Head to **JulieSchooler.com/gift** and grab your copy today.

ABOUT THE AUTHOR

Julie had aspirations of being a writer since she was very young but somehow got sidetracked into the corporate world. After the birth of her first child, she rediscovered her creative side. You can find her at JulieSchooler.com.

Her *Easy Peasy* books provide simple and straightforward information on parenting topics. The *Nourish Your Soul* series shares delicious wisdom to feel calmer, happier and more fulfilled.

Busy people can avoid wasting time searching for often confusing and conflicting advice and instead spend time with the beautiful tiny humans in their lives and do what makes their hearts sing.

Julie lives with her family in a small, magnificent country at the bottom of the world where you may find her trying to bake the perfect chocolate brownie.

facebook.com/JulieSchoolerAuthor
instagram.com/julie.schooler
twitter.com/JulieSchooler

BOOKS BY JULIE SCHOOLER

Easy Peasy **Books**

Easy Peasy Potty Training

Easy Peasy Healthy Eating

Nourish Your Soul **Books**

Rediscover Your Sparkle

Crappy to Happy

Embrace Your Awesomeness

Bucket List Blueprint

Super Sexy Goal Setting

Find Your Purpose in 15 Minutes

Clutter-Free Forever

Children's Picture Books

Maxy-Moo Flies to the Moon

Collections

Change Your Life 3-in-1 Collection

Rebelliously Happy 3-in-1 Collection

JulieSchooler.com/books

ACKNOWLEDGMENTS

I have huge appreciation for the beta readers of this book –
Andrew, Sarah, Kylie, Shona and Karen. I thought you would
spot a few grammatical errors but instead you provided extensive
feedback that has made the book massively better. Thank you!

For championing the 'Rediscover Your Sparkle' concept and
providing constant support and accountability, I am truly grateful
to my friend and business coach, Sally Miller.

To Andrew and our two beautiful tiny humans, Dylan and Eloise.
I live in a perpetual state of astonishment about how fortunate
my life is. Thank you for making me laugh every single day.

PLEASE LEAVE A REVIEW

Rediscover Your Sparkle

Revive the Real You and Be Rebelliously Happy Every Day

THANK YOU FOR READING THIS BOOK

I devoted many months to researching and writing this book. I then spent more time having it professionally edited, working with a designer to create an awesome cover and launching it into the world.

Time, money and heart has gone into this book and I very much hope you enjoyed reading it as much as I loved creating it.

It would mean the world to me if you could spend a few minutes writing a review on Goodreads or the online store where you purchased this book.

A review can be as short or long as you like and should be helpful and honest to assist other potential buyers of the book.

Reviews provide social proof that people like and recommend the book. More book reviews mean more book sales which means I can write more books.

Your book review helps me, as an independent author, more than you could ever know. I read every single review and when I get five-star review it absolutely makes my day.

Thanks, Julie.

REFERENCES

People and Resources

Various TED and TEDx talks, podcasts and blogs

Tony Robbins

Martha Beck

Tim Ferriss

Marie Forleo

Adam Robinson

Elizabeth Gilbert

Derek Sivers

Oprah Winfrey

...and many others

Books

59 Seconds – Change Your Life in Under a Minute – Richard Wiseman (USA, 2011)

Authentic Happiness – Using the New Positive Psychology to Realize Your Potential for Lasting Fulfillment – Martin Seligman, Ph.D. (US, 2002)

Daring Greatly – How the Courage to be Vulnerable Transforms the Way We Live, Love, Parent and Lead – Brené Brown (US, 2013)

Embracing Uncertainty: Achieving Peace of Mind as We Face the Unknown – Susan Jeffers, Ph.D. (US, 2003)

Feel the Fear and Do It Anyway – How to Turn Your Fear and Indecision into Confidence and Action – Susan Jeffers (UK, 1987)

Finding Your Own North Star – How to Claim the Life You Were Meant to Live – Martha Beck (US, 2001)

Finding Your Way in a Wild New World – Reclaim Your True Nature to Create the Life You Want – Martha Beck (US, 2012)

Happy for No Reason – 7 Steps to Being Happy from the Inside Out – Marci Shimoff (USA, 2008)

Heal Your Soul: A Simple Guide to Understanding and Healing Yourself on a Spiritual Level to Create Greater Health, Happiness and Success – Deborah Jane Sutton (US, 2019)

Minimalism – Live a Meaningful Life – Joshua Fields Millburn and Ryan Nicodemus (US, 2016)

Play It Away: A Workaholic's Cure for Anxiety – Charlie Hoehn (US, 2014)

Steering by Starlight – The Science and Magic of Finding Your Destiny – Martha Beck (US, 2008)

The Busy Woman's Guide to High Energy Happiness – Louise Thompson (NZ, 2014)

The Gifts of Imperfection: Let Go of Who You Think You're Supposed to Be and Embrace Who You Are – Brené Brown (US, 2010)

The Happiness Project – Gretchen Rubin (USA, 2009)

The Secret – Rhonda Byrne (US, 2006)

The Seven Habits of Highly Effective People – Restoring the Character Ethic – Steven R. Covey (US, 1990)

The Subtle Art of Not Giving a F*ck – A Counterintuitive Approach to Living a Good Life – Mark Manson (US, 2016)

The Top Five Regrets of the Dying – A Life Transformed by the Dearly Departed – Bronnie Ware (US, 2011)

The Winner's Bible – Rewire Your Brain for Permanent Change – Dr. Kerry Spackman (USA, 2009)

Thrive – The Third Metric to Redefining Success and Creating a Life of Wellbeing, Wisdom and Wonder – Arianna Huffington (US, 2014)

Tools of Titans: The Tactics, Routines, and Habits of Billionaires, Icons, and World-Class Performers – Tim Ferriss (US, 2016)

You are a Badass – How to Stop Doubting Your Greatness and Start Living an Awesome Life – Jen Sincero (US, 2013)

Made in the USA
Middletown, DE
29 July 2024